This book belongs to
Cinnamon's new friend

....

....

Published in the United States by Ink & Willow, an imprint of Random House, a division of Penguin Random House LLC.

INK & WILLOW and colophon are registered trademarks of Penguin Random House LLC.

Interior illustrations: shutterstock.com: **venimo**, decorative border (2184737483); **AutumnStudio**, floral pattern (2065963220); **Zaretska Olga**, flower icons (2195075303), leaf icons (2195809601); acorn icons (2191991733); **Limolida Design Studio**, paw prints (1359743852), apple icon (1968986911), butterfly icon (1968372448), fern icon (2415242297), mushroom icon (2415242297), pinecone icon (2409536535); **ramonparaiba**, tea cup/bread bowl/potted plant icons (2262945041); **Victoria Sergeeva**, shell icon (2320069847); **Natalyon**, sun icon (726165601); **Anton Shaparenko**, hedgehog icon 1 (1489705241); **navegantez**, hedgehog icon 2 (1898567098)

Endpapers: shutterstock.com: **venimo**, decorative border (2184737483); **AutumnStudio**, floral pattern (2065963220); **Anton Shaparenko**, hedgehog icon 1 (1489705241)

Hardback ISBN 978-0-593-58219-0

Ebook ISBN 978-0-593-58220-6

Printed in China

inkandwillow.com

10 9 8 7 6 5 4 3 2 1

First Edition

Cover and interior design by Danielle Deschenes

Cover art: shutterstock.com: **venimo**, decorative border (2184737483); **Limolida Design Studio**, paw prints (1359743852)

Most Ink & Willow books are available at special quantity discounts for bulk purchase for premiums, fundraising, and corporate and educational needs by organizations, churches, and businesses. Special books or book excerpts also can be created to fit specific needs. For details, contact specialmarketscms@penguinrandomhouse.com.

EVERY LITTLE THING QUILL BE ALL RIGHT

HEDGEHUGS AND HAPPINESS
FOR WHEN LIFE FEELS PRICKLY

Ink &
Willow

PHOTOGRAPHS BY AUDRIANNA MARTIN DEL CAMPO

HI THERE!

(From the hedgehog who wrote this book)

Hello, friend!

My name is Cinnamon, and I love snuffling out adventures, trying new things, taking lots of naps, and especially making new friends! This is my first book, and I've written it just for you. Whether you're a hedgehog fanatic or still not quite sure how you feel about spiky little mammals (we're loads of fun—I promise!), you're sure to find something in these pages that quill make you smile.

I may be small, but I have a lot of BIG thoughts and emotions. And from what I've seen of humans, you seem to have a lot on your minds as well. After all, the world is complicated and hard and full of many ups and downs that can make us feel worried, excited, scared, happy, frustrated, overwhelmed, and maybe even a little bit prickly all at the same time. And that's okay. There's a time for everything and a season for every activity (including moments when you want to curl up and hide), which is why I've set up my little book of hedgehugs and happiness into these sections:

- Time to Sniff Out an Adventure
- Time to Forage and Gather Quills
- Time for a Hedgehug
- Time with a Prickle of Friends
- Time for a Hedgehog High Five
- Time to Nest at Home
- Time to Hibernate

Life might be super hard or quilly easy for you right now, but no matter how you feel in this moment, I hope that when you flip through these pages, you'll feel me cheering you on and giving you a hedgehog high five!

Love,
Cinnamon

TIME TO SNIFF OUT AN ADVENTURE

(Because we never know what we might discover about the world and about ourselves when we take that first step out the door)

GET OUT THERE

Sometimes the bravest thing
is taking that first step out of
your comfort zone. And often
the strongest thing is telling
someone you can't do it alone.

FORAGE FOR COURAGE

We're all afraid of something,
but it's how we handle the fear
that makes us brave. And it's the
moments of courage that bring
adventures we never dreamed of.

START SMALL

Whenever the world seems too big for how tiny you feel, focus on the single petal instead of the whole flower. Don't worry about all you have to do. Just remember who you already are.

IT'S THE JOURNEY

If you knew all the answers
today, tomorrow wouldn't
be as much of an adventure.
Because it's not always where
we're going that matters; it's
what we learn along the way.

MIRACLE YOU

You are a walking miracle.
Just wanted to say that in
case you forgot.

TIME TO FORAGE AND GATHER QUILLS

(Because discovering the little things that make us happy can bring some of the sweetest rewards)

ONE QUILL AT A TIME

A life purpose is a big thing to tackle. So instead, focus on each part of your day as it comes. Little by little, the small stuff can make the big things happen.

PRACTICE OVER PERFECTION

Practice doesn't always make perfect, but it does bring fun opportunities and spark potential you didn't know you had.

CROWN OF BEAUTY

You have a lot to offer the world.
After all, you're the only one of
you that has ever been created.

HARVEST JOY

Plant seeds of gratitude
and watch them grow into
wheelbarrows full of joy
and blessings.

MASTERPIECE

You create great things no one else can. So whenever you don't feel confident about picking up your brush, remember that the canvas would be blank without you.

ROOT YOURSELF

You won't really feel like you belong until you do the brave thing of putting down roots. And remember, sometimes the biggest growth happens where you can't see it.

TIME
FOR A
HEDGEHUG

*(Because everyone needs to
be held sometimes)*

FEELING PRICKLY

It's okay to curl up into a ball so that only your prickles show. After all, your prickly parts are as much a part of you as your soft, cuddly parts. Just don't let those prickly spines poke you or anyone else.

SUNNY REMINDER

We're all a little anxious, a little stressed, and a little messed up (or maybe a lot)—but at the end of the day, none of that is who we are. Sometimes we just need a bit of sunshine, a happy flower, or a hedgehug to remind us we are loved.

RIGHT WHERE YOU ARE

When you feel a bit out of place
or even a little stuck, you might
be exactly where you need to be.

FIND REST

Be still and know that you are
loved, you are treasured, and
you are accepted.

MAKE A WISH

Put your wishes out into the
world and see what happens.
Even the tiniest breath of air
can make your dreams go
farther than you ever imagined.

TIME
WITH A
PRICKLE OF
FRIENDS

*(Because life doesn't have to
be perfect when you're with the ones
who know you the best and love you
just the way you are)*

SAFE AND HELD

Some days are chillier than
others, and I end up feeling a
bit prickly. But it's funny how
those are usually the days when
the friends who don't mind my
quills hold me even closer.

LOVE LASTS

If you show someone you love them, you're already winning. "Stuff" won't last forever, but the ways we love and serve others become jewels in an eternal crown.

TRUE GIFTS

Gifts don't always come wrapped
with string. The greatest gift a friend
ever gave me was accepting me
with all my quills. And sometimes the
best gift is just letting someone else
know we're thinking about them.

TABLE FOR FRIENDS

We can gain so much more
than we might keep when
we share what we have.

MAKE SPACE

Loneliness doesn't feel so big
when you have a friend to
join you. So the next time you
feel alone, know that there's
always space for two.

TIME FOR A HEDGEHOG HIGH FIVE

*(Because we were made to celebrate
each other's wins, the good gifts in
life, and every season in its time)*

WINDS OF CHANGE

New seasons, times of change,
and stormy weather are always
easier when you have someone
else holding you up (and a cozy
hat doesn't hurt either).

HELPING HAND

We all need a helping
hand sometimes, and
we can never get too
big to ask a friend to lift
us up when we need an
extra boost.

SHARING MARSHMALLOWS

There's something about a campfire that draws us in and nudges us to share our deep thoughts. And our marshmallows.

LEAN IN AND LISTEN

Lean in close and listen to this:
You're amazing, five thousand
quills, quirks, and all.

ESCAPE

It's a good idea to get away
from it all every so often—
especially when you can
escape to a happy place.

TIME
TO NEST
AT HOME

(Because being cozy is always a good idea and helps us know how to make others feel at home too)

OPEN UP

Home can be a hard place
to open up to others. But the
next time you're afraid to invite
others inside, remember that
the rest of us miss out on the
great and wonderful you when
you keep your door closed.

OUT IN NATURE

On even the spikiest days,
being outdoors can remind
us to take deep breaths. And
sometimes changing our
outer views can help us see
better what's going on inside.

RECIPE FOR SUCCESS

Being passionate is never silly.
It's a good look on anyone.
And when you're free to be
fully yourself, you invite others
at your table to do the same.

BASKETFUL OF FRIENDS

Bringing friends together can be like gathering flowers. Both bring great joy and fill us up.

CUPPA TEA

When everything feels like a little
too much, sometimes the best
plan is to pause and have a cup
of tea. A small break can change
how the rest of your day goes.

TIME TO
HIBERNATE

*(Because we have been created and
called to rest—and because naps are
one of the best gifts in life!)*

TAKE CARE OF YOURSELF

You can't treat others right if you forget to treat yourself. So take care of yourself! You're worth the attention. (And being cozy is always a good idea!)

DOING NOTHING

Sometimes the best thing is
just to do nothing. Especially
when you can do nothing
with the friend who's always
got you.

SLOW DOWN

The spinning in our heads can slow down when we slow our bodies down. So take a moment today to be still and listen to what's going on inside you.

GET COZY

Long day? Need to clear your head? All you need is a warm bath and a cozy blanket, and then everything will be better.

NEW DAY

We begin each
day by opening our eyes.
Every morning is a chance
to start over and see the
world in a new way.

SWEET DREAMS

Sweet dreams, friend. May you find peaceful sleep tonight and awake refreshed and ready to start a new adventure.

FUN FACTS ABOUT HEDGEHOGS

(Like me!)

The name *hedgehog* is a combination of two words related to these little creatures: *hedge,* because they tend to build nests, and *hog,* because of the snuffly snort sound they make.

Contrary to popular belief, hedgehogs are not rodents; they're actually in the mammal order Eulipotyphla!

A group of hedgehogs is called an array or sometimes a prickle.

Hedgehogs are nocturnal and love to hibernate (i.e., take lots of naps).

When hunting or foraging, hedgehogs rely on their senses of hearing and smell, and they can actually see better in the dark.

Known as the gardener's friend, hedgehogs are actually immune to certain types of poisonous plants.

A typical hedgehog has five thousand spikes, which are used for defense.

Even though they're tiny, hedgehogs can travel up to two miles in one go on their little legs.

Hedgehogs were the original animals used as markers for the arrival of spring, but Americans replaced them with groundhogs, which were more prevalent in North America.

FINAL WORDS FROM CINNAMON

Thank you for reading my book! I hope it gave you just the right amount of hedgehog inspiration you were looking for.

My journey of bringing encouragement to others actually began a few years ago. It was an especially prickly set of years for everyone (you might remember which ones I'm talking about), but Audri, my friend and photographer extraordinaire, came up with a creative way of filling the time while also bringing joy to many who were feeling sad and anxious. Teaming up with some of her other artistic friends, she crafted cute scenes starring me and shared them on a dedicated Instagram account. Before this, I'd never been one for the spotlight, but when I realized how much happiness I could share with others, I agreed to help out.

Somehow, our pictures became instantly popular—not only with our own friends but also with lots of new friends we'd never even met! We're both so grateful we were able to inspire people in this way and share hedgehugs all over the world, first online and now with this book.

ABOUT THE PHOTOGRAPHER

AUDRIANNA MARTIN DEL CAMPO
is a professional photographer and
dancer who loves surrealism, storms,
and hedgehogs. She and Cinnamon
make their home in Toronto, Canada.

See more of Cinnamon on Instagram:
@CINNAMON.HODGEPODGE